Praise for Feng Shui Your Life

"*Feng Shui Your Life* offers an easy way to help you shift energy, organize a space, and get things flowing again. If you have read books on feng shui and found them too complicated, *Feng Shui Your Life* is the answer you are looking for."

—YVONNE PERRY, author of *Whose Stuff Is This? Finding Freedom from the Thoughts, Feelings, and Energy of Those Around You*

"*Feng Shui Your Life* is for everyone who wants to feel great in their home. The beauty of this book is that the tips are so simple and easy to do. You will be amazed at how subtle changes, and just a couple of minutes, can truly change your life."

—WHITNEY FERRÉ, author of *The Artist Within: A Guide to Becoming Creatively Fit*

D0188809

Feng Shui
Your Life

Feng Shui Your Life

The Quick Guide to
Decluttering Your Home
and
Renewing Your Life

Tisha Morris

T U R N E R

Turner Publishing Company

200 4th Avenue North • Suite 950
Nashville, Tennessee 37219

445 Park Avenue • 9th Floor
New York, NY 10022

www.turnerpublishing.com

Feng Shui Your Life:
The Quick Guide to Decluttering Your Home and Renewing Your Life

Cover Design: Mike Penticost
Art Direction: Gina Binkley
Author Photo: Courtesy of Zach Goodyear Photography

Library of Congress Cataloging-in-Publication Data

Morris, Tisha.
Feng shui your life : the quick guide to decluttering your home and renewing
your life / Tisha Morris.
    p. cm.
ISBN 978-1-59652-824-6
1. House cleaning. 2. Storage in the home. 3. Feng shui in interior decoration.
4. Orderliness. I. Title.
TX324.M665 2011
648'.8--dc22

                        2011007468

Printed in the United States of America
11 12 13 14 15 16 17—10 9 8 7 6 5 4 3 2

This book is also available in gift book format as
27 Things To Feng Shui Your Home (978-1-59652-567-2)

To all those who have helped me clean house
so that I could find the heart of my home.

If you want to change your life, move 27 things in your home.

~ Chinese proverb

Contents

Introduction

Feng shui is a 5,000-year-old practice that has only been used in Western cultures for as few as 50 years. Similar to when yoga was first introduced to the West, feng shui was brushed off as a New Age fad when brought to the United States by Chinese feng shui masters. However, as more and more people began to apply feng shui, more began to embrace its benefits and experience its power. As they say, the proof is in the pudding.

When I ask people if they know what feng shui is, most are not quite sure. They know it has something to do with their home's interiors and are eager to learn more about this peculiar science. The translation of "feng shui" (pronounced "fung shway") is "wind water," and it was originally used for orienting dwellings in accordance to how the wind and water shaped the land. Today, it is most known for its application to the interiors of spaces. And in our very recent history, clutter clearing—a problem that simply didn't exist in 4000 B.C.—has become a big part of feng shui

The primary purpose of feng shui is to harmonize the energy of spaces with the earth's energy. In doing so, your life will be enhanced in all areas. As a more practical feng shui consultant, I believe the ultimate purpose of feng shui as it relates to homes is to love your home: loving the way your home feels, loving the way it looks, and simply loving every inch of your home. When this is achieved you will start loving every aspect of your life.

When you feng shui your home, you are in effect feng shui-ing your life. Like yin and yang, your home and your life are interwoven and inseparable. In fact, there is a Chinese proverb that says, "If you want to change your life, move 27 things in your home." This proverb speaks of the powerful connection our homes have with our lives. It provides not only words of wisdom but also a breadth of knowledge about the interrelation of energy in our living spaces, known as feng shui.

Many of the suggestions herein are taken directly from feng shui, while others are a modernized version of the ancient art, including clutter clearing. In today's world, clutter has become a major issue that simply did not exist thousands of years ago. Clearing clutter is not only an effective tool for making changes but also an essential one. It is nearly impossible to properly feng shui a house in the traditional sense until the clutter has been cleared. For this reason, the first seven of the 27 things relate to clearing clutter.

It is not only important to clear clutter on the physical level, but on the energetic level as well. Space clearing is another means of making dramatic changes in your home. While clearing clutter refers to clearing out tangible objects, space clearing refers to clearing out the intangibles on an energetic level. This would include clearing old, stagnant, negative energy that may be in your home, whether you are conscious of it or not. Like dirt and cobwebs, negative energy tends to collect in corners, dark areas, behind furniture, and anywhere without proper energy flow.

Space clearing is a subcategory of feng shui that has been used for thousands of years by many cultures, including Native Americans, Mayans, the Balinese, and Hindus. It has become increasingly popular in our modern world. Although the energy in your home is not visible to most people, it is nonetheless very real and affects each of us daily on all levels—physically, mentally, and emotionally.

Like the oxygen flowing through your body, it is important to have a positive energy flow throughout your entire home. Because clearing the energy in your home can have a profound impact on your environment and therefore your life, I have included several methods to properly space clear your home. In actuality, all of the 27 things listed in this book are some form of space clearing. Simply by moving or changing something in your home, you are shifting energy.

There are elements of feng shui throughout these 27 topics. However, the last six of the 27 are some of the more traditional uses of feng shui and are easy to integrate into a home at little or no cost. People around the world have been using these same techniques for centuries because of their steadfast results. Some feng shui applications are scientifically based in harnessing the earth's energy, while others work more mysteriously and are based on the mystical *I Ching,* also known as the *Book of Changes.* Have fun and be creative with these feng shui techniques. You will be amazed at how mysteriously life can work when you allow it.

There are thousands of changes you can make to your home based on design, personal expression, feng shui, or any other discipline or tradition. As an interior designer and feng shui consultant, I find that the lines are often blurred as to which category something falls under. I therefore rely more on my intuition to optimize the look and feel of a space, energetically and aesthetically, while keeping in mind the personal expression of my client. Likewise, use your intuition to guide you. As you read through the following chapters, some ideas will resonate more than others. Keep in mind that the things to which you have the most resistance are also where you may find the most opportunity for transformation.

The 27 things I have chosen are all changes I have personally seen make a profound difference in either my life or the lives of my clients. Some changes will take place immediately, while others will unfold gradually. As the outer beauty of your home unfolds, your inner beauty will be revealed.

Significance of the number 27

Is there something special about the number 27? Yes. It is not coincidental that the Chinese prophet chose 27 for this proverb. Each single digit carries its own unique energy. In numerology, the number 27 holds the energy of the number nine (2+7=9), which relates to completion. And with every completion awaits a new beginning, just as a cycle or chapter in life is completed. Inherent in this completion is change, specifically a change in patterns.

The number nine is also associated with the act of releasing. Change is always the product of releasing the old in order to make space for the new. And inherent in all 27 Things is releasing something—whether it is an item, a perspective, or a belief. Correspondingly, something new will take its place. Even something as simple as changing the color of a room releases the desire for the old color to allow a new color to come into the space.

How to use this book

This book is written for anyone who wants to instantly apply feng shui to their home and, in effect, bring about positive changes in their life. The book is designed to be read from cover-to-cover or to simply pick up on a rainy day, flip to one of the 27 chapters, and start a project. Pick one thing to change or all 27. If you plan to do all or most of the 27 suggestions, I would recommend doing them in the general order they are presented. I have met so many people that want to make changes to their homes, but simply don't know where to begin. For this reason, I have arranged the 27 topics in a logical order. For example, you want to clear clutter before you add energy enhancements. Otherwise, you are just enhancing the energy of the clutter. Similarly there is no point cleaning until after you've moved furniture around, and so forth.

I have also provided in the last section a more in-depth plan to implement all 27 things. This plan will help you to not become overwhelmed. Oftentimes, we dive into a project and quickly feel in over our heads. Or sometimes, we become overwhelmed before ever getting started. If this sounds like you, then I would highly recommend following the plan provided in the back of this book.

One thing to remember is the checklist at the very end of the book. Use it to keep track of your progress. Leave it intact or tear it out and place it on your refrigerator or in a journal. This checklist will keep you accountable for changing 27 things in your home. As you complete one, check it off the list. And as you do, you will see your life change right before your eyes.

Home Is Where the Heart Is

The Chinese people are not the only culture to personalize the energy in their homes. The quote "home is where the heart is" was originally coined by Pliny the Elder during the early Roman Empire, almost 2,000 years ago. The saying is appropriately used to this day because of the inherent emotional and physical connection we have with our homes.

This connection has been recognized in religions, sciences, psychology, cultures, and by our subconscious minds through dreams. The Hindu version of feng shui, called Vastu, may have been the first living science to connect the body and home. Vastu was passed down through a treatise called the Vedas, which also contains the first written information on ayurveda and yoga. In Vastu, the body is said to be a perfect example of architecture. Even in our Western architecture, the human body has been used to determine the basic proportions of spaces, which was the meaning behind Leonardo da Vinci's Vitruvian Man illustration, which was actually used by architect Marcus Vitruvius. Similarly, in Christianity, the body has long been considered a "temple."

Because this connection has spanned the globe for thousands of years, it is not surprising that it has become part of our collective consciousness. Psychologist Carl Jung, along with dream interpreters before him, connected dream symbols pertaining to the house to various aspects of our Self. Dream symbols are archetypes resulting from a collective meaning among masses of people over a long period of time. This is the case with the house. Each part of the house has a correlating symbol relating to our mind or body. For example, windows represent our eyes. It is not coincidental that the eyes are considered the "windows to the soul." This phrase was also used among Christians and dates back to around 50 A.D.

Our home is simply a mirror of our self. A common example of this is how, when the home is messy and in disarray, we may feel mentally disheveled as well. The better your home feels, the better you will feel. And when you feel better—physically, mentally, or emotionally—then life will simply flow better for you. This is the beauty and magic of feng shui. The positive changes you make in your home will be reflected out into your life.

Our home holds all of our energy patterns—the good, the bad, and the ugly. It's challenging to make changes in our lives when we come home to the same energy patterns every day. Have you ever received a great massage or other bodywork, only to slip right back into your negative energy patterns within hours of returning home? Another example is vacations. We come back with new perspectives and inspiration to change our routines and habits, but within a few days of being back we resume our old ways of living. When used periodically, feng shui is like taking a permanent vacation—without the plane ticket.

I
Clean out your closet

It must have been destined for me to be a feng shui consultant. As a child, I absolutely loved to clean out my closet. Or maybe this was just the unspoiled intuition some children have for clearing out spaces periodically. Either way, I still remember that almost euphoric feeling of emptiness once it was cleared out. In hindsight, what I was experiencing in the empty space was the world of new possibilities. It was not so much about clearing out the old stuff as it was allowing space for new things to come in.

And so is the case anytime we clear out anything. Clearing clutter creates space for something new to come in, and what is new can be empowering. As a child, it was the excitement of a new toy, but as an adult, it is the possibility of a new job or relationship. Clutter is anything that no longer serves a purpose that is in your highest and best interest. In other words, clutter is stagnant energy. Clutter takes up valuable space in your home and in your life. Space is our most important commodity. And if you don't take up your own space, your own energy, your own power, then something or someone else will. The clutter in your closet and other areas of your home is indicative of how and where you are giving up valuable space (or time) in your life.

Whenever you feel any stagnation in your life, it's time to clean out your closet. Start with the closet that is most personal to you. This is usually your clothing closet, or the closet closest to your bedroom. This closet sets the tone for everything in your life because you visit it daily. You may think you are only clearing out old jeans, but you are actually shifting energy at a much deeper level. At the same time, don't be surprised if a great deal on a new pair of jeans comes your way. Energy works in very literal ways as well.

How do you know what to get rid of? The rule is that if you don't use it or love it, then get rid of it! There is no point using, wearing, or looking at anything that you don't just love. Life is too short. If you are afraid that you won't find anything better, then you most certainly won't—that is, until you let go of that item. This is true for anything in life. I love to practice this principle with a pair of jeans instead of, say, a job. Try it! You will be amazed. Over time, you will gain the confidence to let go of bigger things in life, only to have something even better return to you.

After you have cleared out your most personal closet, then move on to other closets in your home (and office too). Focus on one closet, or even one section of a closet, at a time so that you don't become overwhelmed. If you think you might get bogged down, then be sure to check out "A Plan to Implement the 27 Things" at the end of the book.

Once you've created some space for new energy in your closet, then move to your drawers and cabinets. Like closets, drawers and cabinets are often a dumping ground for clutter. You will be amazed at the stagnation you will find. This only means a world of possibilities awaits you. And on occasion you may even come across a lost treasure that you had thought was long gone. Again, if this seems overwhelming, then commit to one drawer or cabinet at a time. Once you feel yourself becoming lighter you will be inspired to keep going.

Notes & Ideas

Date: _____

Notes & Ideas

Date: _____

2

Keep doorways clear

Doorways are considered to be "mouths" of chi in feng shui. In other words, doors are the major vessels in which energy, or the "breath," enters and flows through a home, with the front door being the primary "mouth." All other doors are smaller "mouths" that circulate the breath throughout the home. You have most likely experienced how different a house feels when all of the doors are open with a breeze flowing through. Likewise, you can feel the difference in a house with an open floor plan versus a house with smaller, closed-off rooms. You instinctively tap into the energy flow of that space.

Regardless, however, of the quantity of doors in your home, it is essential that each and every doorway be kept clear. There should be easy ingress and egress at each doorway, in addition to the door being able to fully open. Too often we use doors to hide clutter. Even if the door can fully open, do not store anything behind it. Doorways should be clear of anything unless an item, such as a mirror, crystal, or an inspiring picture, is placed there with a positive intention. Doors should also be in good working condition and well lit.

Doorways not only allow for proper energy flow, but they also bring in new opportunities. The front door is particularly related to the opportunities that come into our lives, while the smaller doors relate to making proper, clear decisions relating to opportunities. Cluttered doorways only cloud the decision-making process. Similar to the *Let's Make a Deal* game show in the 1970s, it will become unclear as to whether you should pick Door Number 1, Door Number 2, or Door Number 3.

If you are experiencing difficulties in making decisions or wanting new opportunities to come into your life, then check your doorways. Make sure nothing is impeding their energy flow. If there is, take note of what it is. You may be surprised at how literal the block is. Remove the block. By keeping your doorways clear of clutter, you will walk through new doors of opportunity with clarity and ease. And when opportunity knocks, by all means, let it in.

Notes & Ideas

Date: _____

Notes & Ideas

Date: _____

3
Clear out old pictures

I f you really want to shift energy in your life, particularly in the area of relationships, then clear out old pictures. This is a one-hundred-percent, no-fail guarantee. Pictures hold a vast amount of energy. More specifically, pictures carry the most potent energy of all: emotional energy. As a nostalgic Cancer in the zodiac, I used to think it was an outrage to throw away pictures. In hindsight, I realize it was just my inability to let go of the past.

Pictures are pieces of energy from the past. If you have problems dwelling in the past as opposed to living in the present moment, then clear out old pictures. Clearing out pictures is also effective for cutting the cord with past relationships or memories. By holding on to old pictures, you are hanging on to the past. And while we may want to remember the past, we don't want to be so attached that we prevent ourselves from creating new memories.

Are there pictures from the past that you should keep? Of course. Pictures capture beautiful moments in our lives. They are an invaluable way to remember and pass on the spirit of our friends, family members, and loved ones, as well as places we have been. Pictures have that uncanny ability to speak a thousand words. This is also why it is important that the pictures speak positively. Make sure the ones you keep relate to positive moments and people. If not, consider why you are holding on to them.

Be conscious of what pictures you are keeping. For example, if you just have boxes, or in the case of modern technology, computer files full of pictures, then it is in your best interest to go through them. Discern which ones are worth keeping. Then make those visible through albums or picture frames. Toss out the ones that are associated with negative memories. Burning photos is also an effective way to singe old relationships to which you no longer want to be attached. Most important, create space to meet new people and make new memories.

Notes & Ideas

Date: _____

_____

_____

_____

_____

_____

_____

_____

_____

_____

_____

_____

_____

_____

_____

_____

Notes & Ideas

Date: _____

4

Clean out the basement

If your home has a basement, then you most likely cringed upon reading the title of this section. Nothing brings up more drudgery than the thought of cleaning out your basement. Why? The basement tends to be the place where we store things we don't want to see or deal with. In fact, you may have secretly hoped to never have to see those items again.

In the relationship self-help book *In the Meantime*, author Iyanla Vanzant stresses the need to "clean house," literally and figuratively, from the bottom up before entering a new relationship. She recommends working at the lowest floor first, which in most cases is the basement, because it represents our lowest form of consciousness.

The basement is symbolic of our subconscious mind, particularly those things we have suppressed. If you want to know what you are storing in your subconscious, take a look around your basement. Is it neat and organized? Or is it so messy you don't even know what's down there anymore? Do you store old photo albums or yearbooks? Or are you storing things that you no longer even need? This is often the case with items that, for one reason or another, we have a hard time letting go of. Are you holding on to items that represent an old identity or an old relationship? Or is your basement filled with junk that is subconsciously used as a distraction? These are all examples of emotional clutter.

Like our minds, our basements accumulate things exponentially. You probably even know of someone, perhaps a family member, who would never consider moving just because of the amount of stuff he would have to move, particularly from the basement. In other words, his subconscious mind has debilitated him to the point of complete stagnation. Clearly, it is best to take control of the clutter before it gets to this point. Don't let your stuff take over your life.

In May of 2010, Nashville witnessed what many have called a thousand-year flood. As a result, thousands of basements were flooded. Nashvillians were forced by Mother Nature to clean out their basements. The city looked like a continuous yard sale as thousands of Nashville yards displayed the trash and treasures that had been stored away for years, decades, and in some cases, even centuries in their basements. It looked as though the city had gone through a massive detox.

While the pain, hardship, and economic loss of this event was tragic, I have met so many flood victims who feel like a huge weight was lifted as a result of this purging of clutter. They now realize how little they really need and recognize the physical and emotional burden of storing stuff. Even many in Nashville who did not sustain flood damage became inspired to clear out their clutter.

It is important to note that storing items is not always a bad thing. It certainly can serve a useful and functional purpose. However, it should be done consciously. Be mindful of each item you are storing and, most important, why. Ultimately, the more in alignment your subconscious mind is with your conscious mind, the more in alignment you will be with your true self.

The best way to tackle your basement, or any other overwhelming space, is to divide the cleaning into baby steps and work on one section at a time. Determine what you really need to store and what you don't. Try to be as objective as possible when making this determination. And notice what emotions arise from particular items and whether that emotion is influencing your decision to hold on to something.

Because the basement represents our subconscious mind, it's important that you are conscious of what lies beneath your living space. We often encounter subconscious blocks throughout our day in the form of limiting thoughts, old belief systems, or old identities that obstruct our true desires in life. That box of memorabilia from high school or the passed-down piece of furniture may just be the mine-field that keeps tripping you up.

Notes & Ideas

Date: _____

Notes & Ideas

Date: _____

5
Get rid of unwanted gifts

Number five is probably the most difficult of all the 27 things to complete. We can all relate to not knowing what to do with unwanted gifts. It triggers a deep-rooted emotion: guilt. As a result, we do one of three things with unwanted gifts: stuff them in a closet, display them with distaste and regret, or stuff them in a closet until that gift giver comes to visit.

Unwanted gifts trigger a lot of emotion for people. It is for this reason that ridding your home of them can be extremely transformational. The main reason we do not get rid of unwanted gifts is that we don't want to hurt the other person's feelings. Getting rid of these gifts conjures up guilt, which is the exact reason you need to be rid of them. These guilty feelings also imply a certain level of guilt that exists within that relationship. Getting rid of unwanted gifts provides us with an incredible opportunity to transcend the guilt.

More important, you should love every item in your home. And, yes, even those items stuffed in the closet. Stuffing an unwanted item in the closet is equivalent to stuffing guilt. And then having the unwanted item displayed is a daily reminder of what that gift represents. Unfortunately, there is no simple answer, except to get rid of the item by selling it or giving it away. One option is to set a time limit on how long you will keep the item before getting rid of it. For example, set a one- or two-year limit to keep an unwanted gift before tossing it. Chances are, your time limit will become shorter and shorter over time as you become more conscious of the items you have and want in your home.

Unwanted gifts oftentimes come in the form of inherited items, such as furniture, dishes, and jewelry. I have found that these items are the most difficult for people to get rid of. In addition to the emotional guilt of selling your grandmother's bedroom suit that was handmade by your great-grandfather is the logistics of knowing how to get rid of it. Inherited items usually have or had some monetary worth. I hear repeatedly from clients, "I don't want to just give it away." But then it just ends up being stored in the garage for years with a cloth over it waiting in the wings for another willing family member to take it.

There is no reason to continue passing down guilt through your family tree. Trust me, your deceased relatives will understand! It is your own emotional tie, not theirs. Cut the cord and free yourself. If it's not feasible to sell the item, then find a charity or organization that is near and dear to your heart to whom to donate the item. When a local church was collecting bedding and linens for the orphanages in Haiti, I jumped at the opportunity to donate a quilt from my grandmother that had been collecting dust for years in the linen closet. It was a real win-win for everyone. I felt great about helping the Haitian orphans, I trust that they were able to enjoy the quilt, and I know my grandmother would have been pleased as well.

Ultimately you want to surround yourself only with items and furniture that you love, that resonate with you, and that enhance your daily life.

As always, the best cure is prevention. Ideally, it would be best to not receive unwanted gifts. So be an example yourself. As Gandhi said, "Be the change you want to see in the world." The best way to stop the cycle of keeping unwanted gifts is to be unattached yourself when giving gifts. Also, give gifts that the receiver wants as opposed to gifts you want them to have. If you are not absolutely sure what someone wants, then give them an intangible gift such as a service or an experience gift, or a consumable gift or gift card.

Notes & Ideas

Date: _____

Notes & Ideas

Date: _____

6
Get rid of "just-in-case" items

In my clutter-clearing workshops, it is the "just-in-case" items that seem to garnish the most inner confusion and resistance. Why? Because it goes to the root of trust. Trust in the Universe? Trust in God? No. Trust in yourself.

What exactly constitutes a "just-in-case" item? It is any item that you are keeping just in case a negative condition occurs that is *within your control*. In other words, you are keeping the item because you don't trust yourself.

On one hand, keeping a snow shovel in Tennessee in case it snows is okay. In Tennessee we get a significant snowfall about once every five years. This is a condition that is beyond our control. On the other hand, someone who keeps their "fat clothes" in case they gain weight back after a diet should give their clothes away. The condition is within their control. Understandably, someone losing weight doesn't want to have to repurchase clothes in their old size in case they gain the weight back. But do you really think someone is going to keep the weight off if they already think they won't? Of course not. If someone really wants to maintain their new weight, then getting rid of the old clothes is the first thing they should do.

In a workshop I held with cancer patients, one woman admitted that she was keeping her "skinny" clothes "just in case" her cancer came out of remission. Be conscious of what messages you are sending the Universe. Like a boomerang, they will come back to you. Your belief that you can accomplish something is the single most important part of implementing and maintaining change. According to Lynne McTaggart in her book *The Intention Experiment,* studies using the placebo effect for operations showed that patients who expected a successful operation but did not actually receive an operation fared better than those who had actually received the operation but did not expect a positive outcome.

In another study, scientists discovered the destructive power of having a negative intention. A negative intention has more power to yield a negative result than a positive intention has to bring about a positive result. This is a testament to the importance of the messages we send out. Instead of just saving items for a rainy day, invest in yourself and your belief in a positive outcome. It will be the best long-term investment you can make.

The next time you come across a "just-in-case" item, ask yourself if you really may need it one day. Or is it just an excuse? Determine whether you are setting yourself up for a negative consequence that is within your control. Try to be as objective as possible. I have come across many creative excuses for keeping items. For example, one client in her 60s was keeping a drawer full of hair bands. It was extremely unlikely that she would ever have hair long enough to use the hair bands again. She justified keeping them to use as bungy cords "just in case," but the real reason was that she longed for her youthful long hair.

In another case, a woman was keeping an ice cream maker that she had not used in over 10 years "just in case" she made ice cream again. After digging a little deeper it was revealed that the ice cream maker reminded her of summers with her young children. If you are keeping an item for sentimental reasons, then embrace it. There's absolutely nothing wrong with nostalgia, but don't let it keep you anchored to the past, preventing you from experiencing the present joys of life.

Notes & Ideas

Date: _____

Notes & Ideas

Date: _____

7
Clear hallways and corridors

Hallways and corridors, including stairways, often get overlooked because they are not designated rooms. As a result, they can become a refuge for clutter and neglected items. However, they are as important as veins and arteries are to the heart and lungs. Hallways and corridors are the vessels that feed chi, or energy flow, throughout the home. This is why it is so important to keep them clear of clutter and unnecessary furnishings and objects.

Generally speaking, energy should meander through a space, similar to the air flow throughout your home (and blood flow throughout your body). Hallways and corridors are challenging in this regard. Energy in these transitional areas tends to either rush too much or meander too little. For example, in a long hallway, energy will rush too fast if there is a door or window at the end. On the other hand, energy can become stagnant if a hallway is too dark or clutter-filled. It is advisable to have no furniture in a hallway, unless you need the energy to slow down. If this is the case, then it is acceptable to have a smaller piece of furniture, such as a console table with a light and mirror arranged alongside, assuming it is a wide hallway.

A hallway or staircase should be treated as a room. It can be a great place to hang family photos and artwork. Adequate lighting is extremely important. Unlike most rooms, the hallway has little or no furniture, which makes lighting more challenging. Sconces, recessed lighting, or track lighting are the best options. To help remedy hallways with low lighting, you can paint the walls a lighter color to bring in more yang energy. For hallways with too much rushing energy, try painting them a darker color to bring in more receptive, or yin, energy.

The first thing to do, however, is to clear any clutter, unwanted items, or unnecessary furniture from all of your hallways and corridors. Keep these areas clean and clear and, as a result, the other rooms in the house will get optimal energy flow. You will immediately notice a lightness in your breath and in your body.

Notes & Ideas

Date: _____

Notes & Ideas

Date: _____

8

Change your wall art

Symbols and images are the primary way in which our subconscious mind communicates to us. Unlike our conscious mind, the subconscious is at work 24/7. This is evidenced by our dreams which, not coincidentally, consist primarily of imagery. Advertisers learned years ago that an effective way to program buyers is by using subliminal messages. That is, they flash images in TV ads so quickly that they bypass the conscious mind and instead reach the subconscious mind. According to scientists, the subconscious mind can register a word or image that appears for less than fifty milliseconds. If that is the case, then what about images our subconscious mind is exposed to for minutes, hours, days, or even years?

On a daily basis, our subconscious mind is registering

the imagery on our walls. For this reason, the images por-trayed can influence us greatly without our even knowing it. While our conscious mind may only on occasion notice the painting over the couch, our subconscious mind notices it countless times on a daily basis.

One client of mine had a very beautiful, expensive paint-ing hanging in her living room that depicted a heart with a curving vine shaped like an arrow going through it. She was aware of the imagery and, in fact, was attracted to it when she bought the painting because it replicated the heartbreak she had recently suffered. However, years later, she had for-gotten about the picture hanging and wondered why she was not able to attract a love relationship into her life.

On another occasion a client asked me to feng shui his office. I immediately noticed a piece of art hanging over his desk, a beautiful painting but with startling imagery. It de-picted a sinking ship with an anchor pulling it down under water. When I brought this to his attention, he remarked that he had been feeling like a big weight had been overtak-ing him at work. He had totally forgotten about the picture, but his subconscious mind had not.

What messages are you taking in each day? Take an ob-jective look at the artwork in your home and office. Take note of what conscious meanings each picture has for you. Also consider what symbols the picture may include. For example, animals are highly symbolic and generally have a meaning common to our collective consciousness. Refer to a dream dictionary if you are unsure. Symbols are consistently interpreted by our subconscious mind whether they appear in our waking life or dream life.

Artwork can also alter the energy in a space depending on the subject matter. If you have a room that needs livening up, then add an abstract picture with lots of colors or a cityscape that depicts motion and activity. On the other hand, if you want to create a calm and relaxing environment, such as in the bedroom, use landscapes or abstracts with cool or pastel colors.

Ultimately, all art is completely subjective to the viewer. While a cityscape photo of New York City may be energizing and exciting to one viewer, it may be a depressing reminder of a past experience for someone else. Therefore, the one and only rule of thumb is that you absolutely love every piece of art in your home. Make sure that it evokes positive feelings. If not, then it is time to let that piece go. Replace it with a new piece of art that better represents and expresses who you are or what you want.

Notes & Ideas

Date: _____

Notes & Ideas

Date: _____

9
Hang a vision board

One of the best pieces of art you can hang is a vision board. A vision board is a visual collage of images that represent your desires—what you want, who you want to be, and goals you want to achieve. Vision boards have gained popularity since being featured in the wildly successful book and movie *The Secret*. The premise behind a vision board is that it activates the Law of Attraction, which states that everything in our lives is something that we have attracted, be it good or bad, through our conscious and subconscious desires. Creating a vision board allows you to consciously home in on those things that you want.

A vision board is particularly powerful because of its use of imagery. Because the subconscious mind communicates through images and symbols, the imagery on the vision board speaks directly to your subconscious mind, thereby attracting those things into your life. In addition, selecting pictures and words that are emotionally charged with feelings of desire and passion will speed up the manifestation process even more.

A vision board is both easy and fun to make. In vision board workshops that I hold regularly, we use 20-inch-by-30-inch foam core boards found at any hobby or art store, but you can also use a piece of cardboard or anything sturdy and roomy enough that gives you freedom of expression. Use double-stick tape or craft glue to mount the images. Prior to digging through magazines, take some time to think about what you want.

In my workshops, we feng shui the vision boards according to the Bagua Map, a chart with colored squares representing areas in a house that correspond to areas in life, traditionally used to increase chi within the home (see page 144). Creating your board based on the map will provide a more balanced approach to what you want in your life. For example, instead of the whole board consisting of pictures of your dream home, a feng shui vision board includes desires in all areas of your life, including Career, Love, Knowledge, Helpful People, Creativity, Success, Wealth, Family, and Health.

Once you have considered your desires, start looking for images or words to put on your board that represent those desires. The more specific your desire, the more specific your manifestation will be. Therefore, if you are uncertain about something, then don't put it on the board. "Be careful what you wish for" is apropos with vision boards.

For example, on my vision board I placed a picture of a girl riding a bike just because it was a really cool picture that represented to me the feeling of freedom. That next week, I was strolling through my neighborhood and walked into the local bike shop. I saw a bike that I just loved and the salesman offered it to me for $100 off. It was an offer I couldn't refuse. The next thing I knew I was riding my new bike home! It wasn't until a few days later when I consciously looked at my vision board and remembered the bike picture. My subconscious mind attracted a bike to me even though I wasn't consciously in the market for one. Consequently, the feeling that the image captured for me is the same feeling I get when I ride my new bike.

It is also important that your vision board stay organic. In other words, keep it fresh and flowing. It is perfectly fine to leave empty space on the board and add pictures as you find them. You can always tape over images that have already been manifested, or remove some if you change your mind later. Like the energy in your home, you want to keep it flowing, not stagnant. Also, having fun and being creative with your board is an important step in the manifestation process and thus will allow "good" energy to go into the board.

For a vision board to work most effectively, hang it somewhere visible to you daily. I advise hanging or placing

it somewhere as you would a piece of art. Consider framing
it with a poster frame. Give it the attention it deserves. You
can place it in a public space such as on the mantle in the
living room or somewhere more private, such as a meditation area. Or place it in a room where your desires are most
deeply rooted. For example, if you want to focus on your
career, then place it in your home office. Or if attracting a
love relationship is particularly important to you, place it in
your bedroom. Put your work of art in the spotlight. It will
be the best investment in art you will ever make.

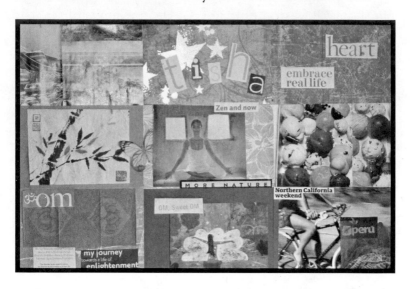

Notes & Ideas

Date: _____

Notes & Ideas

Date: _____

10
Make your bedroom a sanctuary

Although most of us spend more time in the bedroom than any other room in the house, it doesn't always get the attention it deserves. Furthermore, the bedroom oftentimes becomes the room in which we get ready, watch TV, or read the latest novel. Our culture underplays the importance of not only the quantity of sleep we get, but also the quality of our sleep. Your bedroom should be a sanctuary for rejuvenation, romance, and relaxation.

Clean under your bed

At one time or another we have all used the space beneath our beds for storage, especially in a tiny apartment or somewhere with limited space. Although it is very tempting to utilize this space, don't do it! Storing clutter under your bed will cause problems from irregular sleeping to relationship issues to general bad luck. The energy from any items under the bed can affect you during sleep, just as your energy can affect those items. According to traditional feng shui, sleeping over photographs or items associated with family members energetically presses down on their good luck.

Historically, people would keep their money and other valuables under the bed in order to safeguard those items as if it were a bank. It is therefore considered auspicious or lucky to place a symbolic bowl of coins or crystals underneath your bed. Other acceptable items to store under the bed are linens or anything else associated with sleep.

Make sure the area around your bed is also clear of clutter. Too many books, magazines, or electronics can easily disrupt sleep.

Bed placement

The best location for the bed is facing the door, but not directly across, when lying in bed. This position will provide the most peaceful sleep. In addition, notice what the view is from your bed. What artwork or photos do you wake up to? Look objectively at your artwork. Does it represent what you want your romantic life to be? In order to create a more romantic environment, relocate any pictures of children or family members (especially parents), and remove any stuffed animals or any remnants of your childhood.

Bed Placement

a. Best bed placement. You can see the door, but not directly across from it.

b. This is the next best bed placement.

c. Bad bed placement. Chi leaves out the doorway.

d. Bad bed placement. Don't place bed on same wall as doorway.

e. Bad bed placement. Too much chi lfow from doorway.

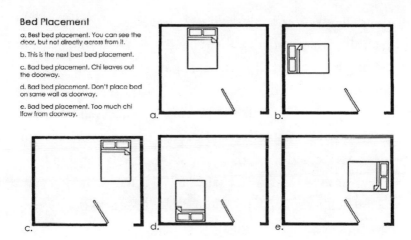

The focal point of any bedroom should be the bed. In fact, if at all possible, the bed and nightstands should be the only things in the bedroom. However, we have gotten away from the original purpose of a bedroom and now use it to store clothing, media consoles, and, God forbid, exercise equipment. Oftentimes, oversized dressers and armoires end up overshadowing the bed. Try to limit the amount of furniture that you place in your bedroom. This will of course depend on the amount of closet space available. Place any objects that have a lot of energy, such as books, magazines, clutter, electronics, and exercise equipment as far from the bed as possible, if not completely out of the room.

If you have one bedside table, make sure there is also one on the other side, along with room to enter the bed from both sides. This equality is important for relationships and for a single person desiring a relationship. In the case of one of my clients, the couple's bed was shoved all the way against the wall with only one of them having access to the bed and the one nightstand. It was clear that one of them played a dominant role in the relationship. I suggested moving the bed away from the wall and placing another nightstand on the empty side. Not only did the room look surprisingly bigger and have better energy flow, but their relationship completely shifted. Having equal entry points to the bed and each having a nightstand had a direct effect on them being equals in their relationship.

Create a sanctuary

Next, consider what colors are in your bedroom. The paint color will dramatically affect the feel of the room. Warm colors, such as beige, brown, pink, red, chocolate, and burgundy are generally better in the bedroom than cool colors, such as blues, grays, and greens. Also, choosing sensual and comfortable bed linens can significantly add to the feeling of the room. For the final touches, add scented candles, sensuous fabrics, and soft music. Whether you are single or in a relationship, it is important to crawl into bed and feel pampered.

The bedroom is the most intimate of all spaces in the home. By making it a sanctuary, you are treating your body, mind, and spirit as a sanctuary and thus treating yourself with the utmost importance, which you deserve. And as you do, your relationship will be a mirror of the sacredness of your bedroom.

Notes & Ideas

Date: _____

Notes & Ideas

Date: _____

11
Paint a room

Anyone who has ever painted a room can appreciate the immediate gratification of change. Painting a room can be one of the quickest and most dramatic ways to aesthetically change a room, not to mention the most bang for your buck. Of course, painting a room can always elicit a change for the worse if the color is even slightly off. We are sensitive to the slightest variations of color.

Color is a very powerful energy that can instantly change our mood. For this reason, there are thousands of books on using color in everything from art to healing to aesthetics. A bright yellow room can make us energetic, while a soft blue room can feel calm and relaxing. Color affects each of us in very different ways depending on our individual disposition. A bright yellow room may make someone angry and irritable, and a blue room can cause someone to feel depressed.

Many times when we feel the urge to change the color of a room, we have had some sort of internal shift ourselves. If nothing else, it is a desire for change. One of the first things people do when they move into a pre-owned home is to change the paint colors. This is a great way to make a fresh start. Painting not only changes the feel of the room but is also a great way to energetically cleanse the room.

The expression "If these walls could talk" can be applied very literally. The walls of a house absorb the energy of its owner. In fact, some people are able to read a home just as others read palms or astrology charts. For example, Karen Kingston, author of *Creating Sacred Space with Feng Shui,* virtually reads the "writing on the walls" from previous owners and teaches others to do the same in her workshops. She says everything that ever happens in a space is recorded in the walls, the floor, the ceiling, furniture, and other objects. Especially susceptible to being imprinted are strong emotions, repetitive patterns, and traumas.

Painting the walls will significantly help to energetically clear this "psychic debris" (except perhaps in the case of significant trauma). Painting with a new color not only changes your emotional response to the room, but it clears away old, stagnant energy as well. This is especially recommended for moving into an older home or apartment that feels dingy. In a place such as this, you are not only picking up on the physical dirt but also on the energetic remains from previous owners. It is no wonder why a freshly painted room feels so clean.

In the case of redecorating, oftentimes simply painting the room a different color is all that is needed. For $50, you can completely transform a room to have a completely different feel. You can change a beige office into a pink baby room. Or turn a bright orange art space into a soft-toned meditation space. Turn a khaki-colored room into a romantic red hot bedroom. Paint a room and create something completely new.

Notes & Ideas

Date: _____

Notes & Ideas

Date: _____

12
Rearrange a room

One of my favorite things to do as a kid was to rearrange my room. I had rearranged my bedroom furniture in as many configurations as possible. I instinctively knew that some configurations were better than others, but it felt good regardless. I would feel renewed, refreshed, and even inspired by the change. Looking back I remember the room looked even clearer and crisper, as if I had just cleaned my glasses. I was, in effect, space clearing.

Even if it is only for the purpose of cleaning, you should move your furniture on occasion. Rarely do we move furniture around as often as we should. We generally move into a space and put the furniture in a place that makes the most sense. It stays there for the next five, ten, fifteen, or twenty years. As a result, energy becomes stagnant under and behind the pieces of furniture during that time. It's usually not until we move to a new space that we are forced to move the furniture. It is not coincidental that moves are often associated with major changes in our lives.

I was recently reminded of the impact rearranging a room can have. Upon moving into my new house, I knew exactly where I wanted the living room furniture. After living with this arrangement for a little over a year, I started to get a little antsy. I bought a new armchair that set into motion a complete rearrangement of the entire living room. I was amazed at how much better the new arrangement was, aesthetically and energetically. This correspondingly set into motion a whole array of new opportunities that began to come into my life.

How does this work? Was it the renewed feeling that I was now embodying and putting out into the world? Was it the fact that, according to feng shui and the Bagua Map, it was the "Fame and Reputation" section of my home? Was it the new flow of energy in the room? It was most likely a combination of all of these.

Our home holds the same energy patterns that are within us. The same energy patterns that allow us to thrive and the ones that cause us to strive. If there is stagnant energy in your home, then there is stagnant energy somewhere in your life, and even in lurking in your body. If you want some shifts to take place, then break up the stagnant pockets of energy in your home. Rearrange a room and you will rearrange your life.

Notes & Ideas

Date: _____

Notes & Ideas

Date: _____

13
Create a sacred space

Build it and they will come" is the phrase that comes to mind when I think of creating a sacred space. Designating a sacred space in your home is essential for anyone who wants to start a yoga or meditation practice. It is also a great area to have for anyone who needs a place to rebalance, recenter, and retreat, which is most likely everyone. Your home in general should feel like a personal sanctuary—a place to retreat to from the rest of the world. Within this sanctuary, designate a space in your home for retreating, centering, praying, and meditating.

This space can be any size—from a two-foot-by-two-foot corner to the size of a yoga mat to an entire room. Designating this space for your personal use is important. Each time you enter that space, you automatically know that you are taking time for yourself. It's similar to the automatic response that yogis have when they hear the word *savasana* (corpse pose) at the end of a yoga class. At first, it's just nice to have a place to retreat. Then, after a while, it becomes a necessary part of your day.

On an energetic level, that space will carry the same energy that builds over time, allowing you to become more peaceful each time. It is no wonder that it is much easier to meditate in an *ashram,* a secluded retreat; the energy has built up over the years to the point that you can step in and immediately quiet your mind and experience peace. The same can be felt in a church or any other sacred space.

Here are a few tips to get started on creating your own sacred space.

Location

Size doesn't matter, but privacy does. Choose a place in your home where you will not be disturbed by people or pets. If it is a shared space with another person or activity, then using a partition rug and screen is recommended.

Clean and declutter

Once you have chosen your location, clear everything out and clean the area of any dust, dirt, or residue. Also clear it energetically with sage or any other herbal cleanser of your choice, such as cedar or sweetgrass. A clear space is a clear mind.

Energize

Next, determine what you want in your space. Perhaps a yoga mat, meditation cushion, a chair, pillows, or blankets. Make it comfortable so that you will want to spend time there. An altar table, whether it is made from a cardboard box or an heirloom piece from India, is highly recommended. In other words, you want to have a centering piece. If space is an issue, then clear off a bookshelf at eye level and make that your makeshift altar space. This space is for placing inspiring and precious objects that are sacred to you.

Personalize

From here, add any items that reflect you and appeal to the five senses, such as candles, pictures, artwork, incense, bells, gemstones, crystals, images, essential oils, affirmation cards, books, and music.

Once you have created your sacred space, sit, relax, stretch, breathe, read, enjoy tea, meditate, or do anything that so inspires you. Treat yourself with this space, and it will create more space in your life by a hundredfold!

Notes & Ideas

Date: _____

Notes & Ideas

Date: _____

14
Paint your front door

If there is one thing that feng shui consultants and real-
tors will always agree on, it is the importance of the front
door. The front door is the main vessel through which en
ergy enters the home. It is also the aesthetic focal point that
creates curb appeal. The front door should be clean, easily
accessible, and in proper working condition. To enhance the
energy even more, paint your front door red. Studies have
shown that painting the front door red will sell a house more
quickly than any other color. Why? It's more eye-catching,
more welcoming, and creates more energy coming through
the door. In feng shui, the color red is associated with vitality, energy, success, and prosperity.

So why wait until it's time to sell your house? If a red
door can positively affect buyers, imagine what it can do for

its occupants. The front door is the primary entry for good chi. This is true even if you don't use your front door as your primary entrance. If you use the back, side, or garage door instead, your front door is still just as important. In fact, it is imperative that you keep the front door active. Use it to go get the mail, take the dog out, or just to let in some fresh air. Otherwise, you are underutilizing available energy for you and your home.

Perhaps a red door does not go with the outside of your home. No problem. Pick a different color. Or if it is a stained-wood door, apply a new coat to make it look new. Either way, give your front door some new energy. Ultimately, the more convivial and welcoming your front door is, the more opportunities and energy will come into your life.

Notes & Ideas

Date: _____

Notes & Ideas

Date: _____

15

Make your least favorite room your favorite

In Eastern cultures, the lotus flower has long been considered a symbol for transformation, enlightenment, and rebirth. The lotus flower roots in the darkest and murkiest waters to transform into a flower with beautiful petals. We see this transcendence occur in other places in nature as well. For example, a purple amethyst stone appears rough, dark, and nondescript on the outside, as does a clam's shell with an exquisite pearl on the inside. A rose comes from a thorny stem, and a butterfly transforms from a caterpillar. It seems as though the darker the origin of a thing, the more opportunity available for transcendence.

And so is the case with your home. Your least favorite room has the potential to become your most loved room in the house. I see this time and time again with clients, usually in the form of a spare room that has become stagnated with hand-me down furnishings or collected clutter. It doesn't necessarily have to be an entire room. It could just be a corner or section of a room that you dislike using or going into for whatever reason. These areas become negative energy magnets attracting more and more each time you walk by, if not through your conscious thoughts, then on the subconscious level.

Step 1: Determine what your least favorite room or area is.

Step 2: Determine what it is about the room that you don't like. Envision what you would like the room to be.

Step 3: Completely clear everything out of the room.

Step 4: Clean the room. Vacuum, mop, dust. Paint the walls if necessary.

Step 5: Create your vision. Only put furniture and items that you love. Be creative.

So where do you begin? First, think about what your least favorite area or room is in your home. For some of you, your least favorite will be just that—your least favorite room. For others, however, it will be a room that you absolutely can't stand to be in. In either case, designate an area that fits your description of "least favorite." The second step is to consider what it is about the room that you don't like. Is it because it's not being used? Does it remind you of something? Is it the bad decor that no longer fits? Is it the buildup of clutter? Pinpoint everything that you don't like about the room.

The next step is to completely clear out the room and remove the stagnant energy. This includes all items and furniture, if possible. This step may take anywhere from thirty minutes to several months depending on the severity of the situation. In clearing the room, consider what furnishings you want to give away or sell. If you need more assistance with this part, then refer to "A Plan to Implement the 27 Things" for specific steps on clearing clutter.

Once you have cleared the room, then it's time to use your creativity to transform it. This could be as simple as changing the function of the room to doing a total renovation. How you change the room should contrast with what you didn't like about the room. For example, if it was a guest bedroom that never got used except to collect clutter, then turn it into a room that you can use for yourself. Use it to explore a new hobby or interest you have. Or if you want to have a guest bedroom for guests to stay in, then make the room more inviting. It is ultimately our intention that creates our future. By creating a room for a particular purpose, this sends out a strong message of what you want more of in your life.

Think about ways you can redecorate to enhance the room. At the least, you should consider giving it a new coat of paint with a new color. This will not only make it feel like a new room, but will also help energetically clear its negative energy. Incorporating new lighting will also make a dramatic difference. I also recommend bringing into the room at least one item that you love, such as a piece of furniture, art, or another object.

It is important to integrate your positive energy into the room. In doing so, you will start to be drawn to the room more and more. Like a butterfly emerging from its cocoon, you will be amazed at how quickly the room will transform into your favorite spot in the house.

Before

After

Notes & Ideas

Date: _____

Notes & Ideas

Date: _____

16
Clean!

Who doesn't love to walk into a freshly cleaned home? You don't have to be a neat freak to appreciate a clean house. While I have always had an affinity for a neat, clean home, a few months ago I experienced a new appreciation for it—I hired someone to clean my home.

I was excited about the prospect of handing over a few chores to someone else, but I was not prepared for a whole new appreciation for a clean home. It wasn't the way the house looked, but the way it felt. My breathing was lighter. My body felt lighter. Even my head felt lighter. It was as if there was an oxygen machine pumping in pure 100 percent oxygen throughout my home. From that day on, I realized the power of cleaning.

The difference in the house being cleaned by me or

someone I've hired is that when I clean it, the cleaning takes place gradually so I don't notice the overall impact. It's similar to cooking, where the chef never appreciates the meal as much as the person eating it. If you do it yourself, the dish may be just as good, but you may not notice it as much. But don't feel like you have to hire someone to clean your house. You can have the same results by cleaning it yourself—just set the intention that you'll appreciate them!

As someone who is sensitive to energy, it is obvious to me that in cleaning out dirt, dust, and debris, the negative energy associated with it gets cleared out as well. It is like getting a massage, which clears away the short-term stress that accumulates throughout the day. It is important to note that you should use as many toxin-free cleaners as possible to get the optimal benefits of an energetic space clearing.

Notes & Ideas

Date: _____

Notes & Ideas

Date: _____

17
Make repairs and improvements

Have you ever felt like you can never get around to making improvements to your home because you are too busy fixing things? In other words, there is so much maintenance that there is neither time nor money left for improvements. This is also the case in everyday life. Sometimes we feel we are just trying to make it through the day, let alone taking steps to improve our lives. For example, it is impossible to train for the half marathon when you've been recovering from an illness. Or, perhaps your yard takes so much time to just maintain that you don't have time to plant new flowers. If this sounds familiar to you, take a closer look at what you have trouble maintaining. And then consider ways in which you may be able to simplify your life to lessen your load.

When items are broken, in disrepair, or not working properly, then there is an inherent disharmony present. This discordant energy disperses throughout your home in a wave-like fashion, affecting other areas of the home and, most important, its inhabitants. This especially includes furniture. For example, if you sit at a wobbly desk every day, you will eventually suffer leg or foot problems. For an item that is broken or in disrepair, it is important either to fix it immediately, give it to someone who can repair it, or discard it appropriately. This applies to anything from furniture to electronics.

Making necessary repairs around your home is extremely important for the energy in your home. As you make repairs in your home, you are accordingly making repairs to yourself. Likewise, as you make improvements to your home, you will intuitively begin some aspect of self-improvement. Do unto your home as you would do unto yourself!

Notes & Ideas

Date: _____

Notes & Ideas

Date: _____

_____

_____

_____

_____

_____

_____

_____

_____

_____

_____

_____

_____

_____

_____

_____

18
Clean your windows

Want more clarity or a new perspective in your life? Just as eyes are the windows to the soul, windows are our eyes to the outside world. Windows not only bring in light and connect us to the outdoors, but they are also an important contributor to the overall energy in homes. Windows increase chi, or energy flow, and should therefore be kept clean and clear. Cloudy windows are equivalent to cloudy water. For example, think of how different a fish tank looks with clear water versus cloudy water, not to mention the difference in the overall feel of the room the tank is in.

If you wear glasses or contacts, then you know the sudden clarity you had the first time you put glasses on. This is the same with the windows in our homes. We oftentimes need a new perspective in life. When you find yourself in such a situation, try cleaning your windows. By seeing clearly into the outside world, you are able to see beyond yourself with a new clarity and objectivity. This can also help in making clear decisions and paying attention to the details of life.

Notes & Ideas

Date: _____

Notes & Ideas

Date: _____

19
Space clear with sage

Space clearing is another important branch of feng shui. Although clearing clutter certainly contributes to breaking up stagnant energy, space clearing fine tunes the energy in a space as well as energizes it. The difference in a room after it has been cleared is palpable. Even my clients who are unfamiliar with detecting subtle energies can feel an immediate difference once I have space cleared their home.

Why space clear?

Although most people cannot see energy, it is nonetheless very real. Everyone has had the experience of "picking up" another person's energy. The expression "You could cut the tension with a knife" refers to how we can almost tangibly feel energy. Every one of us has an energy field, or aura, that surrounds our body. Our energy field emits and takes in energy, which then gets assimilated through our endocrine system. As a result, we can "feel" and sometimes even "take on" other people's moods.

The emotions that we emit and that are emitted by others linger in our homes and often become stagnant energy. This is a major reason why regularly clearing your home's energy is so important. According to Karen Kingston in *Creating Sacred Space with Feng Shui,* everything that happens in a space goes out in ripples, similar to that of a stone being dropped in a pond. The energy then becomes imprinted on the walls, floors, furniture, objects, and people in the space. Furthermore, any events eliciting strong emotions or trauma are recorded with more intensity, while repetitive patterns become deeply imprinted as well.

When we move into a home, the first thing we instinctively do is clean the space. No one wants to live with the previous owner's dirt. But what about their energetic baggage? In addition to cleaning the space, it is important to energetically space clear it as well. You may have seen patterns of houses within your neighborhood where everyone who has lived there gets divorced, immediately moves, files bankruptcy, or gets sick. This is because of the energy patterns that are in place. While these may be extreme examples, you certainly don't want the fate of previous owners to determine yours.

And then there is our own energy that we bring into

the space on a day-to-day basis. We all have bad days, argu-
ments with loved ones, illnesses, and emotional upheavals.
This energy can become trapped, so to speak, in your home
as well. And like a big energy magnet, the same negative
emotions will be more likely to arise in the occupants again
and again. By periodically space clearing your home, you
can prevent this from happening. You can live life in the
present moment on a clean slate instead of being subjected
to the default energy patterns in your home.

How to space clear

There are many different ways to space clear, or purify, a
space. Since the goal of feng shui is to live in harmony with
the earth, space-clearing methods usually take the form
of the four primary elements—fire, water, air, and earth.
Burning sage would be an example of using a fire element
to purify a space. Different cultures use different methods
in accordance with their traditions. Using a sage stick, also
known as a smudge stick, is a tradition borrowed from Native Americans and now used worldwide as a space-clearing
technique.

A smudge stick, available in natural health food stores,
metaphysical shops, and online, consists of a bundle of
herbs. Sage, usually the primary herb, is often mixed with
other herbs such as lavender, cedar, and sweetgrass. Simply
light the end of the stick like incense and begin waving it
around the room.

Energy is most stagnant in corners, behind furniture, and in nooks and crannies. One rule of thumb is that where dirt and cobwebs lurk, so does stagnant energy. For this reason, I recommend starting at the perimeter of a room, working around the room, and ending up at the center. While walking around the room with the stick lit, hold an intention of clearing the room.

Once you have finished and the smoke has dissipated, look around the room. You will notice that the room looks crisper and the colors appear brighter. You will also notice immediate benefits from clearing your home that will positively affect your health and well-being. You will be able to breathe more deeply. You will feel much lighter.

I recommend space clearing your home once every few months, or sooner if you feel an urge. I typically space clear after giving the house a good cleaning. For periodic space clearing, it is advisable to do on your own. In cases of trauma, serious illness, presence of ghosts or spirits, or other extreme cases, then it is recommended to hire a feng shui consultant or other space-clearing professional.

SPACE-CLEARING TECHNIQUES

- Start with the perimeter of room and end in the center.

- Work your way around the room with sage or bells.

- Pay close attention to the corners. Similar to dirt and cobwebs, this is where stagnant energy hangs out.

- Also focus on corners or areas that are not exposed to natural sunlight.

- Be present and place your intention on clearing the room. Be as general or specific as you want with your intention.

- Space clear furniture, especially antiques. Plants love space clearing too!

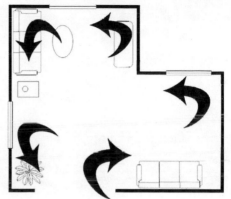

Notes & Ideas

Date: _____

Notes & Ideas

Date: _____

20
Ring some bells

In addition to sage, sound is also an effective way to clear energy. In fact, some believe that using sound is the most powerful space-clearing technique because it produces an immediate vibrational shift in the room. Sound methods used for space clearing include bells, drums, cymbals, singing bowls, and even clapping.

Sacred sounds have been used throughout history. For example, ancient Chinese theaters would use clapping as a way to invoke the presence of gods prior to stage performances. This was incidentally adapted by Western culture as clapping at the conclusion of a performance. Bells and gongs have been used regularly in churches and monasteries. The use of bells and horns is referred to throughout the Bible as far back as the Old Testament book of Exodus, written around 3,500 years ago, which mentions gold bells worn on priestly clothing during worship. In the Hindu religion, the Sanskrit word *om* is said to be the original sound that created the Universe and is often used in chants. Drums and rattles have been used ceremoniously among Native Americans to dispel negative energy and to call in the Spirit World.

Regardless of what instrument or source of sound is used, it will be effective for space clearing. Sounds create a harmonic resonance. For example, whether you use Tibetan bells or a chime for space clearing, your home and all the energy contained therein will attune to the necessary frequency, resulting in a harmonic balance throughout. The effect of the sound will ripple throughout the space long after human ears can actually hear the sound. It is best to use bells made from base metals, such as brass, silver, copper, lead, or tin, to activate the yang (active) energy.

To space clear with a bell, stand in the center of the room. Upon the first strike, notice the quality of the sound. This is indicative of the energy in the room. As you continue, the ring will become more consistent and less wave-like. Eventually it will sound crystal clear. Continue doing this as you walk around until the entire room has a clear sound. If you have multiple bells, then start with the largest, or deepest, bell, working your way to the smaller, higher-pitched bells that fine tune the energy.

If you are feeling tired and lethargic, then the energy in your home is too, and vice versa. Bells will revitalize and reenergize your home. Sound has a life force all unto itself. Use the bells to periodically clear your home and create your own sacred space full of life and vitality.

Notes & Ideas

Date: _____

Notes & Ideas

Date: _____

21
Add a crystal

Crystals are true "gems" in feng shui. They are small but mighty, inexpensive but invaluable, and often irregular in shape but in perfect harmony. Crystals bring an energetic balance to a room that only nature can provide. Crystals can remedy virtually any feng shui malady you may have. They can be hung in a window to energize a room, placed on a table to harmonize a room, or suspended from the ceiling to slow down or speed up energy in a room.

Crystals of any size can be used. It is important, however, to purchase real crystals, not imitations made of plastic. Round, faceted cut-glass crystals are often used in feng shui to disperse light and energy in a room. When crystal contacts light, it will refract the light like a prism.

Crystals should be cleaned periodically, as they absorb

negative energy. Simply run them under water with the intention of cleansing them. Another method for recharging crystals is to allow them to soak a few hours in the sunlight or overnight in moonlight.

Crystals and gemstones are also effective for bringing in good luck to areas of your home. In the succeeding chapters you will learn where in your home your Wealth and Prosperity and your Love and Relationships corners are. Place a crystal in each of these areas to help energize them. An amethyst is particularly auspicious for bringing in wealth, whereas rose quartz can be used to bring in more love.

Each time you use a crystal in your home, set an intention for that crystal. Like a recorder, the crystal will remember your intention and assist you in manifesting your specific desire.

Notes & Ideas

Date: _____

Notes & Ideas

Date: _____

_____

_____

_____

_____

_____

_____

_____

_____

_____

_____

_____

_____

_____

_____

_____

_____

22
Add a mirror

What is considered to be the Band-Aid of feng shui? That's right—a mirror. It seems that if my clients know anything about feng shui, it's that mirrors should be used. But rarely are they sure just how and where. Mirrors amplify, expand, and circulate the energy in your home. In fact, mirrors can activate the chi, or energy, in a space so intensely that it is possible to overactivate a space with mirrors.

Take a moment to think about where you currently have mirrors in your home. Of course, we all have mirrors in bathrooms and vanity areas. Does the mirror cover the entire wall above the sink or is it a smaller, hanging mirror? Think about how you feel in that room in correlation with the size of your mirror. Do you find yourself rushing to get ready? Or do you have problems feeling energized? In the 1980s, the decorative trend was to mirror entire walls with high-wattage lighting to boot. This was indicative of the fast-paced, high-energy eighties generation. The current trend is hanging mirrors with softer lighting while bringing in more natural elements.

In what other rooms do you have mirrors? Mirrors are a great way to make a small room seem bigger, or make a hallway seem wider. They can energetically make a wall disappear as if it is a window. Another option is to hang a mirror across from a window to increase the light and the perception of space.

It is important to notice what a mirror is reflecting. Is it hung too low so that you cannot see your head? Or is it reflecting only part of an object, making it look distorted? Remember: whatever the mirror is reflecting is what is being enhanced. It is therefore important that mirrors themselves are not cracked, warped, or distorted.

The following list will help you to properly place mirrors in your home or office.

Do place mirrors in rooms to increase energy and activity, such as in the living room, bathroom, kitchen, and office.

Don't place mirrors in rooms dedicated to rest and relaxation, such as bedrooms and dining rooms. Never place a mirror across from a bed.

Do use clean, clear glass mirrors that realistically reflect whole images.

Don't use cracked, broken, decoratively pieced, or purposely distorted mirrors that misrepresent the image being reflected.

Do hang a mirror to reflect a window.

Don't hang a mirror to reflect another mirror.

Do place a mirror to reflect a beautiful piece of artwork or fireplace mantle.

Don't place a mirror to reflect an area of clutter.

Do face a mirror in the direction of unwanted obtrusions, such as power lines or noisy neighbors. It will reflect back on the obtrusions instead of into your home.

Don't place a mirror to where you can see unwanted views of neighbors, sharp corners, or traffic.

Notes & Ideas

Date: _____

_____

_____

_____

_____

_____

_____

_____

_____

_____

_____

_____

_____

_____

_____

Notes & Ideas

Date: _____

_____

_____

_____

_____

_____

_____

_____

_____

_____

_____

_____

_____

_____

23
Integrate the Five Elements

Walk into a beautifully decorated model home or even your favorite room in the house. What you will find is a natural interplay of the Five Elements: Wood, Fire, Earth, Metal, and Water. The Five Elements are considered the basic building blocks of everything on the earth and within ourselves. It is only natural that we feel best in environments with a harmonic balance of these essential elements. This is one reason why nature feels so good to us. Nature naturally strikes a balance between the Five Elements.

Some people have a natural affinity with design and will intuitively harmonize a space using the Five Elements without even realizing it. For example, most interior designers and decorators who are not adept at feng shui will naturally incorporate the Five Elements into a room. One important thing to know about the elements is that each one has certain shapes, colors, and qualities associated with it. These aspects can be seen in everything in a home, from fabrics, artwork, and accessories to furniture, materials, and appliances.

The use of each element will naturally differ depending on what materials are readily available in certain regions. For example, in the South, most new homes are brick, whereas in the North, most homes are constructed of wood. In the Southwest, adobe is the material of choice due to its availability and climate adaptability. It is therefore important to find creative ways to incorporate all five elements into a space. Let's take a look at the characteristics associated with each of the Five Elements.

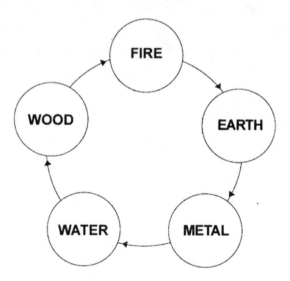

Wood

The Wood element is probably the most common element in interiors. Wood is used in furniture, flooring, support beams, columns, picture frames, cabinetry, doors, walls, and even as an exterior material. A log cabin is an example of an overbalance of the Wood element; another is a basement with wood-paneled walls. Although these spaces can provide a warm, cozy feeling, they can also become too much of a good thing after a while. Examples of the Wood element include:

- Anything made of wood, including furniture and materials
- All plants and flowers, including fake plants
- Artwork depicting landscapes, flowers, trees
- Most fabrics such as cotton, silk, rayon
- Columnar-shaped objects
- Shades of green and blue

Fire

Naturally, fire is not as prevalent in our homes as wood, but it can be found coming from a candle, incense, a fireplace, or a stove. However, there are numerous other ways to incorporate the Fire element into our living spaces. Here are some examples:

- All lighting, including artificial and natural light
- People and pets
- Textiles or accessories made of fur, leather, wool, feather, or bone
- Triangular or cone-shaped objects
- Shades of red
- Artwork depicting any of the above

Water

The Water element is inherently a feminine aspect of energy, also known as yin energy. On the other hand, the Fire element is naturally a masculine aspect of energy, known as yang energy. Balancing aspects of fire and water in a space is a particularly auspicious combination of a yin-yang balance. This is often seen with fountains that contain a candle or light in the center. Although fountains are the most obvious example of the Water element in interiors, here are some more that may not be so obvious:

- Glass, mirrors, crystal, reflective surfaces
- Bowl-shaped, flowing free-forms
- Black or dark-toned colors

Earth

The Earth element is most commonly found and associated with elements of the Southwest. It is found in materials such as brick, tile, and adobe and in accessories, including ceramic or terra cotta pots. Here are some other ways to integrate the Earth element into a room:

- Pottery, ceramics
- Images of the Southwest, earth landscapes, deserts
- Long, flat surfaces such as squares and rectangles
- Earth tones such as yellow, orange, brown

Metal

Actual metals are used throughout the home in various ways. Stainless-steel appliances are very popular. Wrought-iron or metal stairwells are used often, and silver and gold are incorporated through accessories. My experience with the Metal element is that it doesn't take much of it to make a big impression. Here are some examples:

- Any type of metal
- All rocks, stones, and gemstones, including granite, marble, slate
- Crystals and gemstones
- Sculptures
- Circular and oval shapes
- White, light colors, and pastels

With this basic knowledge of the Five Elements, anyone can enhance a space and create positive energy. Go to your favorite room or area and see what Elements are present. Also notice if there is a dominant Element throughout your home that you gravitate towards. Based on Chinese Medicine principals, we all have a dominant Element within us. And this usually shows up in our homes as well. For example, do you have a lot of items made of glass, or wood, and so forth? Try mixing in aspects of the other Elements with it. You may be surprised by what you see and feel.

Notes & Ideas

Date: _____

Notes & Ideas

Date: _____

24
Enhance the lighting

Without light, there would be dark. While this sounds obvious, it is an understated concept in interiors. Without light, you would not even be able to see the wall color, let alone your beautiful artwork. Lighting is the most important aspect of any interior space. It is essential for aesthetics, feng shui, and function. You could spend thousands of dollars on a room, but without proper lighting, it simply will not shine. On the other hand, a room in need of a makeover may simply need a $39.99 floor lamp to completely transform it.

Lighting can be extremely mood-altering. Grocery stores with blaring fluorescents change my mood instantly. Compare that with walking into a softly lit restaurant. Although some people are more sensitive than others, lighting affects everyone on a subconscious level. Businesses, particularly retail stores, are well aware of this effect and have begun to incorporate better lighting into their spaces. In fact, according to studies, businesses accustomed to focusing on products, services, and salesmanship are now focusing on atmospherics, with lighting being the main attraction. In offices, employers are finding that lighting plays an important role in productivity. Lighting is also being used more effectively in public spaces, such as airports and hospitals.

In order to improve or enhance the lighting in your home, it is important to note the different types of lighting.

Natural light

Ultimately, all artificial lighting attempts to replicate natural sunlight. Homes and rooms with doors and windows have a natural advantage. Nothing beats the feel of seeing natural morning light trickling through the front door and reflecting off the floor, or watching the sunset through the kitchen window. In rooms blessed with natural light, very little artificial lighting is necessary, at least during the daytime.

It is possible for rooms to actually get too much sunlight. Light is considered to be yang energy in feng shui. The Yin Yang symbol is synonymous with balance. If a room has too much light, or yang energy, then it needs to be balanced with yin energy. Simply put, blinds or window coverings may be necessary, particularly in the summer or in hot climates where sun is plentiful.

Task lighting

Task lighting is the light that helps you read a book, see the recipe and chop the vegetables, and see the paper to write on. Task lighting is the light that makes tasks easier, its main purpose being function. It is the reading light, the spotlight over the sink, and the drafting lamp. But despite its functional purpose, there is no reason your task light needs to be boring. Make it part of the look and feel of the space too.

Ambient lighting

Ambient lighting is the closest to replicating natural light. It provides the most general light in a room, which also makes it the light that can make or break the feel of a room. Examples of ambient lighting include the overhead light in the center of the room and recessed lights scattered on the ceiling.

For rooms with no overhead lighting, ambient lighting can be produced with an array of table lamps or floor lamps. For rooms with one overhead light, use a table or floor lamp either instead of or in tandem with the overhead light. Using one overhead light directly in the center of a room will make the room appear one-dimensional and downright depressing. There are exceptions, of course, such as a crystal chandelier.

Accent lighting

Accent lighting is the key to providing depth and dimension to a room. It is the secret ingredient! Use accent lighting to illuminate cabinets, to create drama with uplighting or downlighting, to spotlight art, or to alter the feel of a room with a dimmer, tinted lightbulb, or fixture. An accent light can completely transform a space. It can highlight the favorable aspects of a room or create a mood of your choice—all with the flip of a switch.

It is worth mentioning the importance of lightbulb selection. Using a different bulb may be all that is necessary to positively affect a room. For example, I had a client whose home office did not feel right to him. His office was in the basement with no windows. This was the first clue that lighting was going to be essential. I looked up and saw that he had replaced the recessed halogens that had burnt out with fluorescent bulbs. I immediately knew that this was the primary source of his problem, which was confirmed when he told me that he often suffered from headaches.

Fluorescents have been praised and even required in some states for their energy efficiency. However, they come with disadvantages as well. From an environmental standpoint, they contain a vaporous form of mercury that can be extremely dangerous to the environment if not recycled properly and, not to mention, if accidentally broken at home. Fluorescents are better in some ways than the traditional incandescent bulb, but still not the final answer.

Another problem with fluorescent lighting is that it can produce what is known as the "flicker effect," a low-frequency flicker that affects approximately 10 percent of the population and results in headaches, drowsiness, and inability to concentrate. Even if you are not subject to flicker effect, fluorescent lighting can negatively affect the feel of your space. Consider using halogen or full-spectrum bulbs instead.

Manufacturers are quickly working to improve fluorescent bulbs and now have a tinted version that emits a much softer light. Advances are also being made with LED lighting. The bottom line is to be conscious of what lightbulb is being used. Purchasing a different bulb may solve your lighting problem rather than buying a new lamp or replacing a fixture.

Decorative lighting

Decorative lighting can add a sparkle to any space. It can come in the form of a unique artisan-made light bought from a local artist, a glass-blown lantern bought on vacation, or a candle set on the fireplace mantle. Decorative lighting is more about decoration than the actual light emitted. It can be great for personal expression or to add an exclamation point to a room.

Notes & Ideas

Date: _____

Notes & Ideas

Date: _____

25
Stimulate the senses

Like a good story, a room should stimulate all five senses. It's obvious that a space should look good, but what about sound good, smell good, and feel good? A well-designed space should always engage and stimulate all of the senses. Let's take a look at each one.

Sight

A beautiful piece of art encapsulates elements of design in order to engage, while being easy on the eyes. A room should do the same. In *The Artist Within*, Whitney Ferré points out that the eight elements of design—emphasis, balance, proportion, unity, harmony, rhythm, contrast, and repetition—should be present not only in art but also in life.

This is also true with each room of our home. According to Ferré, the principles of design are the "language of our mind's eye," and how we visually analyze everything we see.

Our eyes are automatically attracted to these design elements. For example, a room should have a focal point, such as a fireplace mantle with a favorite piece of art, candlesticks, and vases symmetrically placed on each side. Your eyes will then naturally travel around the room, noticing a repetition of shapes or colors, perhaps then finding a contrasting color in a throw pillow. Our eyes love to see these elements, and when they are in play, they "unleash the artist's potential inside our brain," says Ferré.

Pick a room in your home and approach it as if it's a piece of art. Be creative with ways in which you can integrate the eight elements of design. For ideas you like, browse through home decorating magazines. See what elements of design catch your attention the most, then emulate those in your own home. A good balance in art "parallels being well-rounded in life," says Ferré.

Smell

For people with a sensitive nose, this category is a no-brainer. Smells can make or break a potential love relationship, or your patronage of a store or restaurant. The sense of smell is powerful. In fact, the body can distinguish around 10,000 different scents. It is our most primitive sense and the one most associated with memory. As scents are inhaled, the smell travels along the olfactory nerves in the nose and then up into the part of the brain that controls mood, memory, and the ability to learn. When this area is stimulated, it releases endorphins, neurotransmitters, and other "feel-good" chemicals. In other words, smells can make us feel really good or really bad.

For this reason, aromatherapy has become increasingly popular. Not only does it make a room smell good, but it also elicits physiological changes, such as relieving stress, improving mood, boosting the immune system, improving memory, and stimulating blood circulation. It is commonly used in holistic and wellness centers and also in hospitals. For example, an oncologist at the University of Texas Anderson Cancer Center in Houston, Texas, uses aromatherapy to assist in treating cancer patients.

Aromatherapy is likewise a great way to enhance a room. Although aromatherapy is technically the use of plants and herbs in an oil base, the term is generally referred to as any enhancing scent from candles, incense, and oils. Electric or candle-based oil diffusers can be used to heat and circulate oil scent in a room. Or you can simply light a candle or burn some incense.

If you want a relaxing feel, try lavender, clary sage, geranium, sandalwood, or rosemary. To invigorate a space, try using peppermint, jasmine, tea tree, ylang ylang, or eucalyptus. High-grade essential oils are recommended over chemically produced scents.

Remember that smells correspondingly stimulate our

sense of taste—think of the aroma produced from baking cookies or fresh bread in the oven.

Sound

Sound can quickly and dramatically change the feel of a room. Music is the most obvious example. Clearly, playing classical music, soft jazz, or rock music will greatly alter one's mood. Public spaces are often defined simply based on the music played.

A more subtle way to incorporate sound is with wind chimes. Chimes and bells generate a pleasant sound and are able to energetically clear a room. Chimes are also used in feng shui to generate chi in a room (even if they are just hanging there!).

Other ways to stimulate the ears is with a sound machine, a fan, children's laughter, a fountain, or singing. The worst sound is produced by a television, which releases electromagnetic waves that over time can cause fatigue, depression, and headaches.

Touch

A room with a variety of textures will stimulate the sense of touch. For example, a leather couch paired with a soft cotton blanket and a wooly rug make a great combination because of the varying textures. Think of when you go into a showroom or furnishings store. Probably without even thinking about it, you run your fingers along pillows, couches, fabrics, and furniture. Like children, we want to experience things through touch. Pair different textures together in your home to create a feast for the senses. In doing so, you will make the rooms feel amazing.

Notes & Ideas

Date: _____

_____

_____

_____

_____

_____

_____

_____

_____

_____

_____

_____

_____

_____

_____

_____

_____

Notes & Ideas

Date: _____

26
Add pink to enhance your love life

In feng shui, the Bagua Map is the quintessential tool used to determine which areas of the home represent which areas of life. Originating from the *I Ching,* known as *The Book of Changes,* the Bagua Map (also referred to as the Pa Kua) has been used across continents for thousands of years. According to feng shui masters, the energy of the Bagua Map is present in a home, or virtually any space, whether you are conscious of it or not. The Bagua Map is a tool used to enhance your life by increasing the chi in each area of a house, including the Love and Relationships corner. This area is used not only to cultivate new and improved relationships with others but with yourself as well. It is a beneficial aspect for everyone.

How to use the Bagua Map

Abundance & Prosperity	Fame & Reputation	Love & Relationships
Family & Community	Mind Body & Health	Creativity & Children
Wisdom & Knowledge	Career & Life Purpose	Helpful People & Travel

front entrance

The Bagua Map is a square with nine sections, like a tic-tac-toe board, that you lay over a sketch of your home's floor plan. It is malleable to fit your floor plan, so if your home is linear or shotgun-shaped, then the Bagua Map would also be shaped like a long rectangle.

Each square represents a certain area of your life, with the top-right corner representing Love and Relationships. If you are standing at your front door looking in, then the most upper-right corner of your home is where this area lies (see diagram). This corner of your house may be a room, part of a room, or multiple rooms depending on the layout and size of your home. In addition to the Love & Relationships corner, you can use the Bagua Map pictured above to see where the energy correlating to other areas of your life falls within your home.

Once you have designated the Love and Relationships area of your home, it is now time to enhance the energy there. First, take note of what is in that area. Is it cluttered? Is there a piece of furniture there that you don't like that could be a "block"? Or is it one of your favorite rooms in your home? Notice if the feeling or tone of the room correlates with the current state of your relationships.

The next step in improving the corner's energy is to clear any clutter in that area. Refer to any of the previous sections on other ways to enhance the energy flow in this area of your home.

Step 1: Check for any items that could be an energetic block. For example, check for clutter in this area, particularly items that bring up emotions from the past or past relationships.

Step 2: Clear out *any* clutter.

Step 3: Energize this area of your home with pink, a crystal, or any of the other suggestions mentioned in this book.

Add some pink

Finally, incorporate pink somewhere into the Love and Relationships area of your home. (Yes, even if it is the garage.) Every Bagua Map square is associated with a particular color that was not arbitrarily selected. Each represents a color of the light spectrum that emits a different frequency, or vibration. In other words, colors are energy.

Pink is the color that holds the frequency of love. You can incorporate pink into this space on any level—from painting the walls pink to displaying a rose quartz to just putting a piece of pink construction paper in a drawer. No one except you even needs to know that pink is in the room or why it is there; the only requirement is that as you incorporate pink into the space, you also have an intention in doing so. In other words, have an intention with what you would like in this area of your life. It could be to meet someone new or to strengthen a current relationship. Using your intention in conjunction with the energy of the Bagua Map will give you the best results.

This is the diagram for adding pink:

		L&R

Notes & Ideas

Date: _____

Notes & Ideas

Date: _____

27
Add purple to bring in wealth

The Wealth and Prosperity corner is another common area of the Bagua Map, located in the top-left corner. From your front door looking in, it will be the top-left corner section of your home.

Working with the Wealth and Prosperity section of your home is a great way to bring abundance into your life. This could be in the form of money or anything else of which you want more. For example, one client of mine discovered that her kitchen trash can was right in her Wealth and Prosperity corner. She completely cleaned and cleared out the entire area, relocated the trash can, and made the space an altar with items she loved, including a purple amethyst. Consequently, the next day she received unexpected good news from her accountant!

Once you have designated the Wealth and Prosperity section of your home, it is now time to enhance the energy in that area. Notice what condition that area of your home is in. Is it cluttered? Is it a bathroom where the toilet lid is open or a trash can is present? If so, do you feel like your money is going down the drain? Take the necessary steps to alleviate any negative energy that may be present in this area. Declutter the space. Remove any items that may be causing stagnation. To promote growth in this area, place healthy plants or anything alive and energetic there.

And finally, add purple to your Wealth and Prosperity corner. As pink is to love, purple is to prosperity. To promote this prosperity, add hints of purple to this area of your home or decorate the entire room in shades of purple. Place an amethyst stone in a window sill or add a purple throw pillow. Be creative. And always have an intention in mind. Each time you enter the room, your subconscious mind will pick up the energy in conjunction with your intention and start attracting more wealth and prosperity. Try it. You have nothing to lose and everything to gain!

This is the diagram for adding purple:

W&P		

Notes & Ideas

Date: _____

Notes & Ideas

Date: _____

_____

_____

_____

_____

_____

_____

_____

_____

_____

_____

_____

_____

_____

_____

_____

A Plan to Implement the 27 Things

At my first feng shui workshop, I was excited to share my passion with people wanting to learn about feng shui. I prepared endlessly and provided my audience with two hours of useful information in the form of examples, worksheets, stories, and facts that seemed well received. At the end, one woman appearing a bit overwhelmed raised her hand and simply asked, "What should I do first?" I paused for a moment and thought, "What a great question!" Since then, I have worked on a step-by-step plan to help people implement the most effective changes for their home. In fact, this has become the cornerstone for my workshops.

In implementing the 27 things in this book, I have divided them into four phases, each one logically following the next. Before going forward, however, there are a few important rules that should be followed along the way.

Suggestion 1: Work in baby steps

Whether it took one year or twenty years to create a basement full of clutter, don't expect to clear it out in an hour. Setting unrealistic goals is the number one reason people give up on clearing clutter. Instead, break up the job into small steps. For example, in taking on a monumental task such as cleaning out the basement, dedicate a few hours or a few days to one corner or section. If you are cleaning out closets, then focus on one at a time. Same with drawers—focus on one chest and break it down into each individual drawer.

Keep in mind that clearing clutter is as much about the quality of energy you are clearing as it is the quantity. For example, selling a Civil War gun collection that has been passed down to you or getting rid of a photo album from a past relationship may be as important as cleaning out every drawer and closet in your home. Those things that are the hardest to get rid of also hold the most energy for you. Upon letting go of them, a vast amount of space is opened up, allowing new things to come in.

Suggestion 2: Be present

As you go about doing any or all of the 27 things, be present. Whether it is clearing cobwebs from the corners or discarding old photos, be conscious. Listen. You may be surprised at what messages come through or what emotions or memories come up. Objects, like humans, have energy fields that carry energy and associated memories. If an object stirs you up emotionally, don't push aside the emotions. Most likely that object has been stored somewhere for years, just as the emotion has been stored in your body. Instead, explore it, feel it, release it, and then cut the cord with that item. Once you are finished, be present and notice how you feel. You will be amazed!

Suggestion 3: Have an intention

One way to become more present is to hold an intention of what you want to accomplish. Your intention can be as general or specific as you want. It may be to make your bedroom cozier, to create more space in your closet for new clothes, or to attract a new relationship. Where intention goes, energy flows.

Human intention is one of the most powerful energy forces on Earth. When coupled with the earth's energy or chi through feng shui techniques, you can exponentially transform your home and life. The power of your mind in along with the actual shifting of energy is a magical combination. So make the most of the time you are putting into your home, and you will see the fruits of your labor harvest with even more abundance than you can imagine. Now you are ready to get started!

Suggestion 4: Being green while decluttering

We thankfully live in a time when we think twice about throwing something away. Unfortunately, the feeling of contributing to a landfill, however, may prevent you from decluttering altogether. In keeping with the Reduce Reuse Recycle rule, here are some ways to be green and declutter so that saving the earth will no longer be your excuse from saving yourself.

Reduce. The best thing about clearing clutter is that once it's gone, once you realize just how much you have accumulated and how little you really need, then you are so much less likely to consume as much in the future. *Clearing clutter reduces future consumption.* In fact, after clearing out your clutter, you will feel so much lighter that you will not want to re-clutter your space. And when you do get the itch for something new, you will be oh-so-much-choosier in what you purchase.

Reuse. The second tier of being green is to Reuse. The best way to reuse items is to give them away. Make it a regular practice to keep a give-away bag or box around for taking to Goodwill or a similar organization. Just make sure that these items are reusable and not items that should be in the next category: recycle. For example, your favorite sneakers from 1988 that have holes and worn-out souls should not be reused. Freecycle.org is another great way to have your items reused. Just list your item and have someone who needs it come and pick it up for you. For any items that you want to sell, consider listing them on craigslist or eBay.

Recycle. Now that you have pared down your items to those no longer reusable, it's time to recycle. So many more items are recyclable than you may think. If you don't already recycle paper, glass, aluminum, and plastic on a regular basis, then start now. Every major city has recycling centers, if they don't already pick up at your home. Research what services your city already offers.

For those items that are not obviously recyclable, check out www.earth911.org. Earth911 is your one-stop source for finding out what you can recycle and where—from mattresses to computer monitors to eyeglasses. Simply search by your zip code. It's incredibly easy and informative.

So instead of feeling guilty about adding a printer to the landfill, consider whether it is reusable and, if not, recyclable. Before long, you will automatically be reducing. The best thing is that it feels good to be green *and* clutter free.

The plan

Most of us walk into a room, see a disaster zone, and have no idea where to begin. The feeling of being overwhelmed soon turns into apathy, and apathy turns into abandoning the project altogether. Instead, try following this plan, broken down into the following four phases:

1. Remove clutter,
2. Change things up,
3. Clean and clear the space, and
4. Invigorate with feng shui elements

Each of these phases can be used with any space, whether a drawer, a room, or the entire house. Remember, it is best to work in baby steps and to keep in mind quality, not just quantity. Be present and have an intention.

Phase 1: Remove clutter

- Clean out your closet
- Keep doorways clear
- Clear out old pictures
- Clean out the basement
- Get rid of unwanted gifts
- Get rid of "just-in-case" items
- Clear hallways and corridors

The first step is to remove clutter. In the list of 27 things, this includes items 1 through 7. Get rid of what no longer should be in the space. This is one example in which less really is more. There is no point in moving around furniture that you're not going to keep, not to mention that it is physically much easier to clean a space with less in it. It is also essential to clear clutter before incorporating the traditional feng shui techniques. Feng shui is based on harmonizing and optimizing the flow of energy within a space, which is simply not possible if clutter is stagnating a room's energy flow.

Clearing clutter has become one of the most popular offshoots of feng shui. It has become an art within itself, with many helpful books on the topic. If clutter is an Achilles' heel for you, then consider exploring this topic more. That being said, it is usually just a matter of doing it. And to get around to doing it, you must first make it a priority by setting aside time to clear the clutter.

Clearing clutter can be broken down into the following four-step process: 1) Set aside time; 2) Sort into piles; 3) To keep or not to keep; and 4) Delivery.

Set aside time. For many, clearing clutter can be overwhelming, which is why it has accumulated to begin with. We put it off and just let stuff collect. So the first step of clearing clutter is to make time for it. Make it a priority. To do this, create a block of time in your schedule. For example, take a day off from work or carve out an afternoon, or simply designate the next thirty minutes for clearing clutter.

At the same time, if and when you get a spontaneous urge to clear something out, go with it. I find that this is when I am most productive. This urge usually means that there is something on the emotional level that I am also clearing out in my life. Clearing clutter can be an instinctive process, and it can be an intuitive step for self-growth.

If you are someone who needs more structure, then you will need to set out a personal plan for yourself. Make a list of all the areas you want to clear out, along with how long each area will likely take. Then set a reasonable goal for accomplishing each one. If needed, reward yourself upon each accomplishment. However, you will find that the best reward will inherently be the cleared space.

Sort into piles. Make sure you have on-hand boxes, plastic bags, a recycling bin, garbage bags, and permanent markers for labeling. This step is important because you don't want to clear one closet just to shift it all to another closet. While you are clearing, you want to be able to immediately place the items in their destination to reduce any further clutter. If you do place them somewhere temporarily, make sure it is only temporary. Set a goal for when you will have the items removed permanently.

As you start the clearing process, it is helpful to sort the items into the following piles or sections:

- Trash
- Recycling
- Returns
- Donations
- For sale
- Undecided

For trash items, place in trash bags. For recycling items, place in a recycling container immediately. For returns, place in a designated box. For items that will be donated, place in an appropriate bag or box for immediate delivery. For the items you have designated for sale, whether it be for a garage sale, craigslist, or eBay, make sure the item is worth your time to sell. Make sure you are not using the "for sale" items as a way to distract yourself into keeping them. Save the undecided pile for last, as it is the most difficult. It's now time to determine whether to keep or not to keep those items.

To keep or not to keep. Knowing what to keep and what to get rid of is the essential question that arises when clearing clutter. As a reminder, clutter is anything that no longer serves your highest and best interest, regardless of monetary value. A $200 crystal bowl can be clutter if it was a gift you don't particularly like but feel guilty getting rid of. On the other hand, a piece of scrap paper with an inspiring quote may not be clutter.

Clearing clutter is a very subjective process that ironically requires a great deal of objectivity. In determining what to keep, ask the following questions:

- *Do I use it?*
- *Do I love it?*

You should love or lovingly use everything in your home. If you don't, it is taking up valuable space.

For those items that you either can't make your mind up about or just can't part with, ask yourself why. You will find a deeper meaning, and perhaps then you will be able to part with them. If not, then save them for the next round of clearing. However, the emotional weight will eventually get to you. Just like everything in life, we hold on until it becomes easier not to. Each time you clear clutter you will be amazed at how much easier it gets and how much more you can part with. In fact, it becomes extremely freeing. When you successfully do it once, you realize life really does continue without a particular item.

Delivery. This step is as crucial as the first step. There is no point in going through your items, just to put them in a box in your closet. Instead, immediately take the trash and recycling out. Deliver the donation items within 24 hours, along with any items to be returned. Begin the process for selling the items to be sold.

This final step can be the most annoying, but also the most therapeutic. Once you have properly rid yourself of the items, you will feel so much lighter. It can also be more time-consuming than you think, so build in plenty of time for appropriate disposal.

One of the biggest payoffs from clearing clutter is that you will be much less likely to accumulate clutter in the future.

Phase 2: Change things up
- Change your wall art
- Hang a vision board

- Make your bedroom a sanctuary
- Paint a room
- Rearrange a room
- Create a sacred space
- Paint your front door
- Make your least favorite room your favorite
- Enhance the lighting
- Make repairs and improvements

Once you have cleared the clutter out of the space, then it's time for the fun part. Paint a room, rearrange the furniture, add new lighting, or even build on a new addition. Turn the spare bedroom into a yoga or hobby room. Carve out a section of your home office for a sacred space. Or make your bedroom a place for romance and rejuvenation. Be creative. Pick one or all of the changes in Phase 2. Take some time to look at your home objectively with new eyes. See what changes would benefit your home and you.

Consider the overall function of each room in your home and how often it gets used. If you never use a room, think of something creative to do with that room. For example, if you have a guest room that never gets used, then turn it into something else more functional. Or if there is a room in the house that you just don't like going into, consider why. Perhaps it just needs better lighting or rearrangement. Love every room of your home, and make your home a sanctuary you love coming home to.

Phase 3: Clean and clear the space

- Clean!
- Clean your windows
- Space clear with sage
- Ring some bells

The value of a good cleaning cannot be understated. Physically cleaning a piece of furniture, a room, or the entire house can do wonders. Cleaning out the dust and dirt is removing more than just dust and dirt. It is the psychological removal of anything no longer in your best interest. We collect cobwebs in the corners of our minds just as we do in our homes. By tangibly removing them, you are doing the equivalent mentally.

Once you have finished physically cleaning the space, it is time to energetically clear the space. By now, you have removed the stagnant energy from clutter, the old energy from the dirt and debris, and sufficiently moved furniture around to also stimulate the energy flow. Using sage, bells, intention, and any other method that feels natural to you, clear the space—in corners, behind furniture, and anywhere else lacking proper energy flow. In addition, any areas in which negative emotions have been released or where someone with a physical illness has been should also be energetically cleared.

It is best to use sage and lower-pitched bells first for clearing the space. Then follow up with a higher-pitched bell to invigorate the space.

Once a space has been cleared, invoke positive energy in the form of love, positive affirmations, prayers, a blessing, and an intention. Light a candle or some incense as an offering or blessing to your home.

Phase 4: Invigorate with feng shui elements

- Add a crystal
- Add a mirror
- Integrate the Five Elements
- Stimulate the senses
- Add pink to enhance your love life
- Add purple to bring in wealth

Now that you have cleared your home of clutter, moved things around, and completely rid it of stagnant energy, it is time to invigorate the space with positive energy and intentions. According to Denise Linn, founder of the Interior Alignment technique and author of *Sacred Space,* once you have cleared the stagnant energy in your home, fill it up with "radiant light and crystal-clear energy." Otherwise, says Linn, it would be like "cleaning out a flower vase but never putting fresh flowers into it." Phase 4 is like adding the flowers to the vase.

These feng shui elements will put the finishing touches on your home. Some will visually enhance your home, while others will energetically lift the space. In either case, the result will be the same: your home will feel great, and so will you.

The last two things—adding pink and purple to certain areas of your home—utilize the Bagua Map. The map (Pa Kua) is used to show what areas of your home represent different areas of your life. I have selected the two most commonly enhanced areas, love and money, but there are seven other sections of the map.

For a more detailed exploration of the Bagua Map, I would recommend the *Feng Shui Your Life eWorkbook* or the feng shui iPhone app that I developed, called "Feng Shui Bagua Map."

Invigorating your home with these feng shui elements is an opportunity to put your personal stamp on your home. It should not only be a visual reflection of yourself, but an energetic expression as well. Your home should feel good to you and be a place where you love to be. As you love your home, you will also love yourself.

27 Things Checklist

Phase 1: Clear clutter

- ☐ Clean out your closet
- ☐ Keep doorways clear
- ☐ Clear out old pictures
- ☐ Clean out the basement
- ☐ Get rid of unwanted gifts
- ☐ Get rid of "just-in-case" items
- ☐ Clear hallways and corridors

Phase 2: Change things up

- ☐ Change your wall art
- ☐ Hang a vision board
- ☐ Make your bedroom a sanctuary
- ☐ Paint a room

- ☐ Rearrange a room
- ☐ Create a sacred space
- ☐ Paint your front door
- ☐ Make your least favorite room your favorite
- ☐ Enhance the lighting
- ☐ Make repairs and improvements

Phase 3: Clean and clear the space

- ☐ Clean!
- ☐ Clean your windows
- ☐ Space clear with sage
- ☐ Ring some bells

Phase 4: Invigorate with feng shui elements

- ☐ Add a crystal
- ☐ Add a mirror
- ☐ Integrate the Five Elements
- ☐ Stimulate the senses
- ☐ Add pink to enhance your love life
- ☐ Add purple to bring in wealth